Going to the Dentist

A TODDLER PREP™ BOOK

Ready
SetPrep

Copyright © 2022 Phase 2 LLC

Toddler Prep™, ReadySetPrep™, and associated trademarks are owned by and used under license from Phase 2 Prep LLC.

All rights reserved. No part of this book may be reproduced or used in any manner without written permission of the copyright owner except for the use of quotations in a book review. For more information, contact author.

All characters and events are products of the author's imagination, and any resemblance to actual events, places or persons, living or dead is entirely coincidental.

Special thanks to Kacie M. Culotta, DMD

About Toddler Prep™ Books

The best way to prepare a child for any new experience is to help them understand what to expect beforehand, according to experts. And while cute illustrations and fictional dialogue might be entertaining, little ones need a more realistic representation to fully understand and prepare for new experiences.

With Toddler Prep™ Books, a series by ReadySetPrep™, you can help your child make a clear connection between expectation and reality for all of life's exciting new firsts. Born from firsthand experience and based on research from leading developmental psychologists, the series was created by Amy and Aaron Pittman – parents of two who know (all too well) the value of preparation for toddlers.

We're going to the dentist! It's important to go to the dentist because they help our teeth stay clean and healthy.

There will be so many new things to see and do. Let's talk about what happens when we go to the dentist.

When we get to the dentist's office, we go inside and check in at the front desk.

Then, we sit and wait for your turn. There are lots of chairs inside the waiting room.

Sometimes, the waiting room has books and toys. You might see other kids waiting for the dentist, too.

When it's your turn, the dental hygienist calls your name and takes us to the back. The dental hygienist is the dentist's helper.

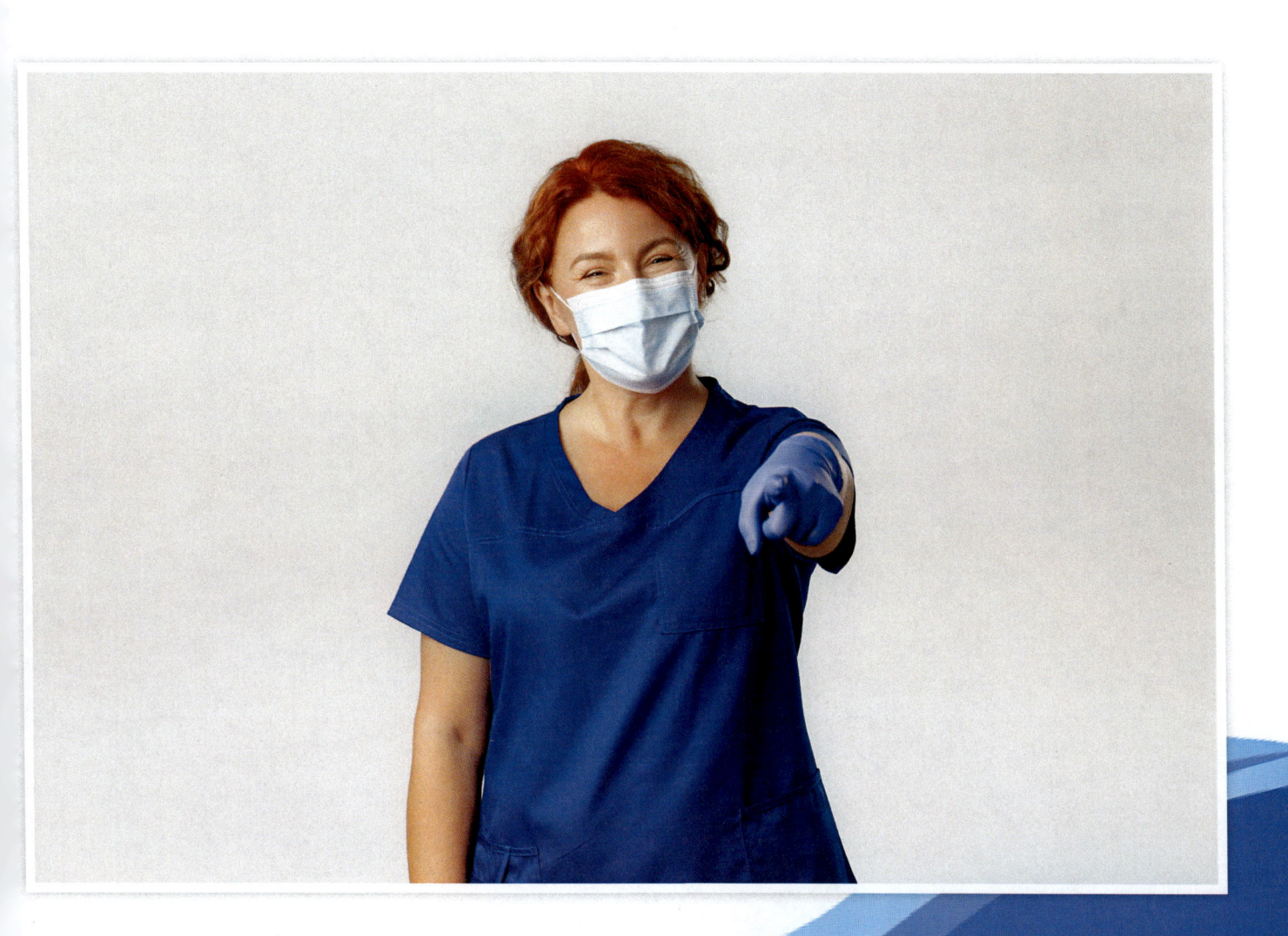

Next, we go into the exam room. Inside there is a special chair for you to sit in and lots of instruments for the dentist to use.

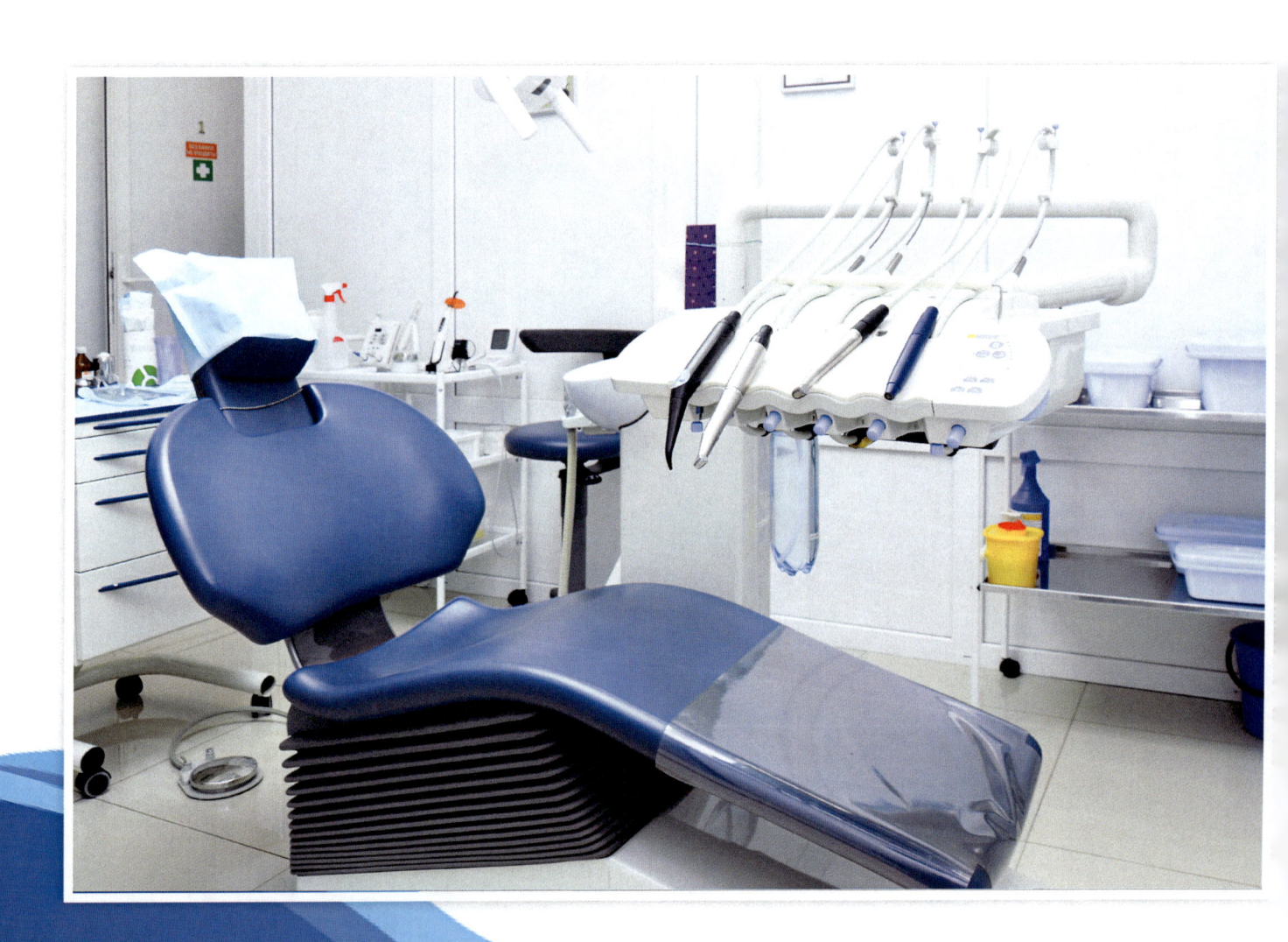

The chair is really fun. It moves up and down and you get to lay all the way back.

When you lay back you see a bright light. The light is for the dentist to see inside your mouth.

You get to wear cool sunglasses to protect your eyes from the light, and a bib to protect your clothes from splashes.

To start, the dentist looks in your mouth with a little mirror to count all your teeth. I wonder how many teeth you have?

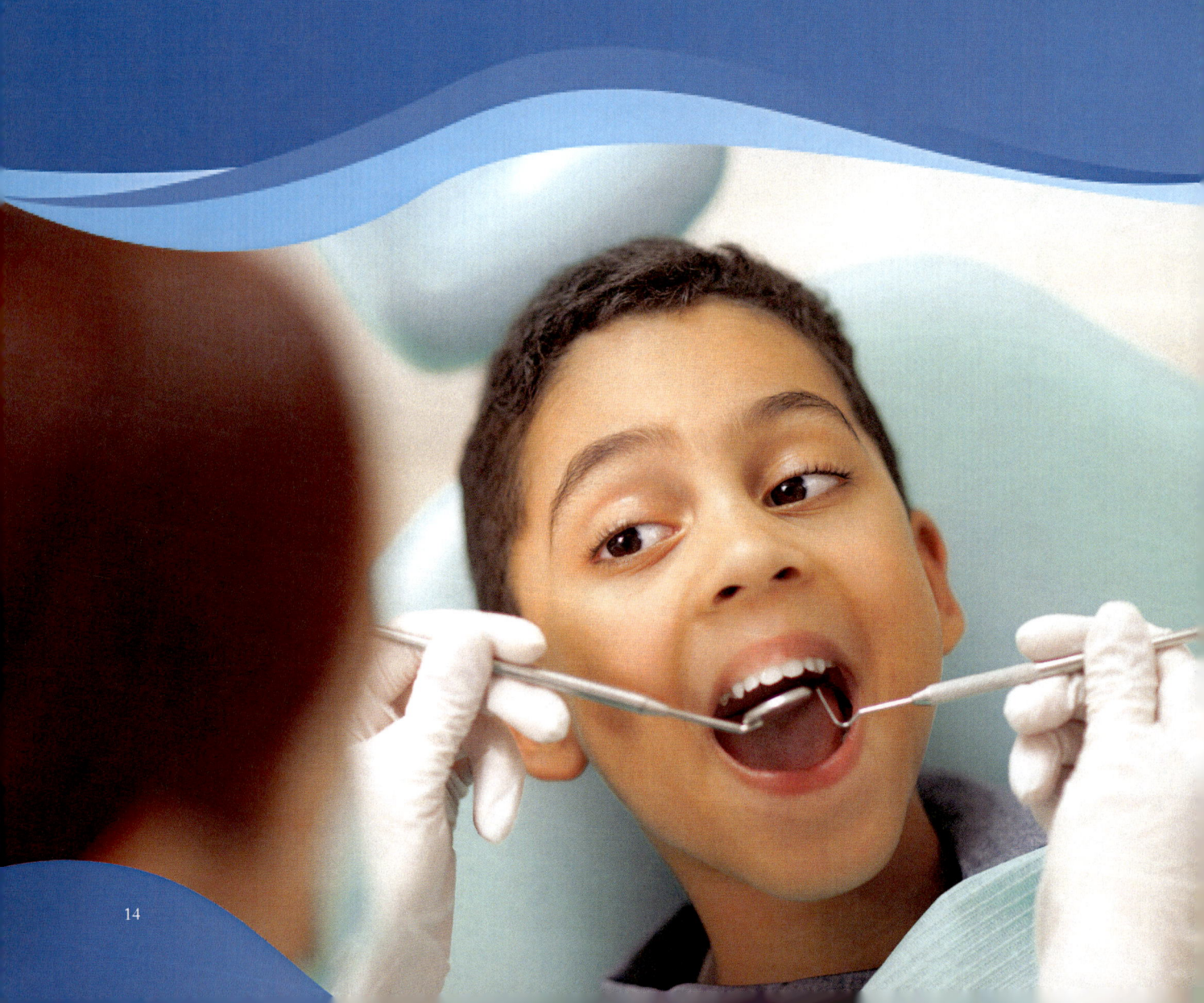

They will also use a pointy tool called an explorer instrument. It looks sharp, but it doesn't hurt when they use it.

Then, the dentist looks underneath your lips and tongue.

Sometimes, the dentist uses a camera to take pictures of your teeth. Say "cheese!"

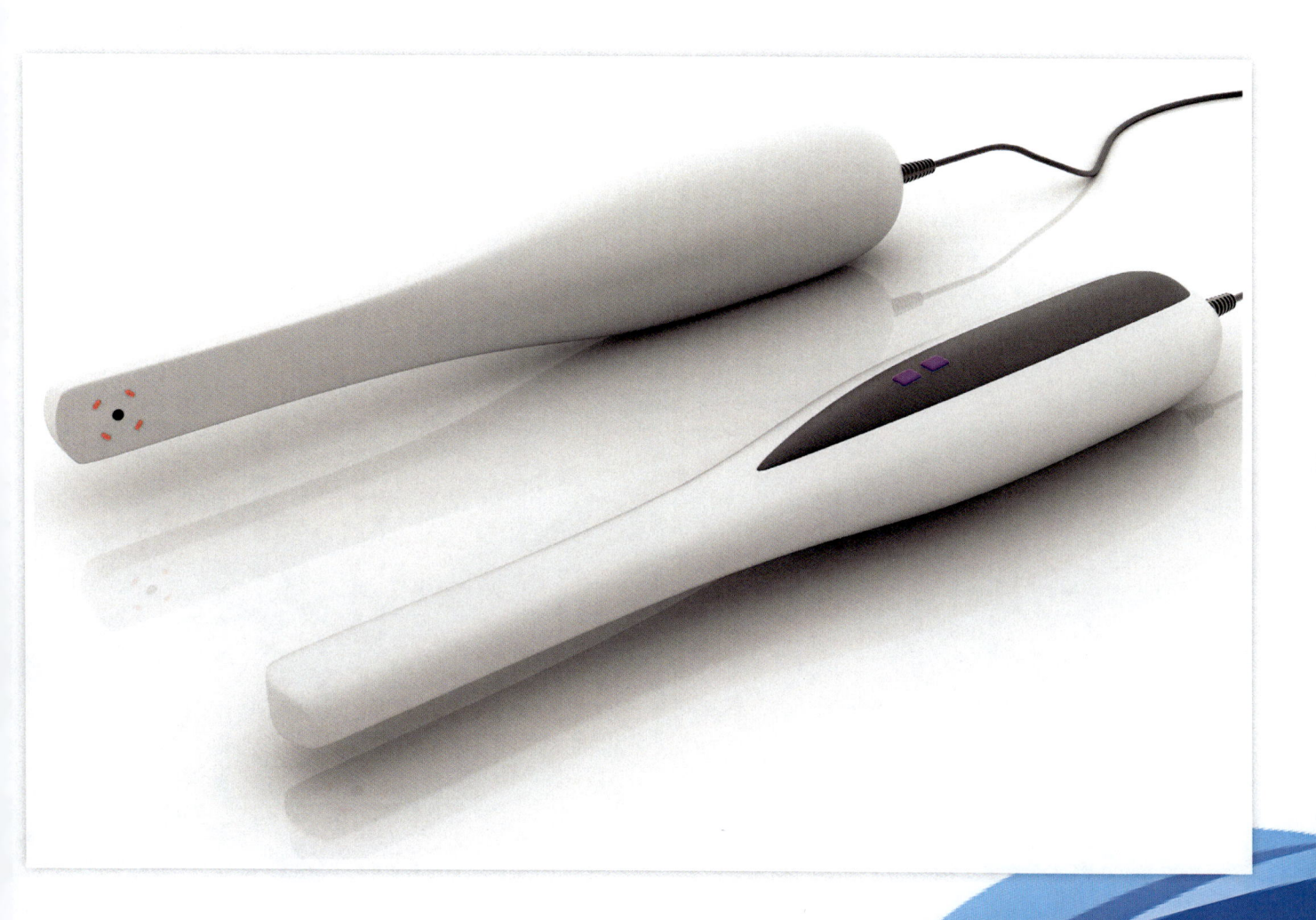

After the pictures, the dentist uses a scaler instrument with a little hook that cleans off plaque. Plaque is where germs live on your teeth.

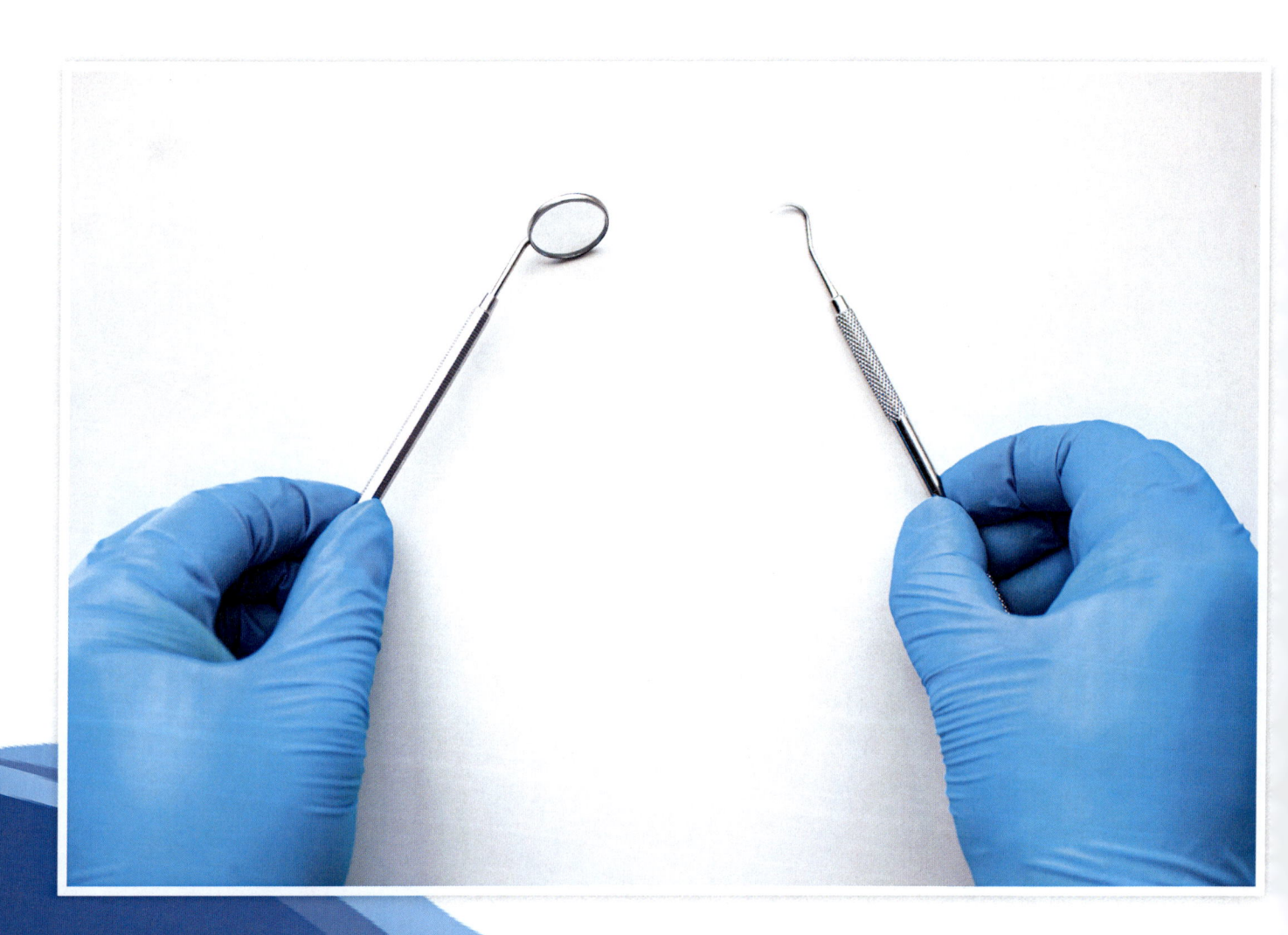

Now it's time to pick your favorite flavor of toothpaste. They might have strawberry, mint, or even bubblegum!

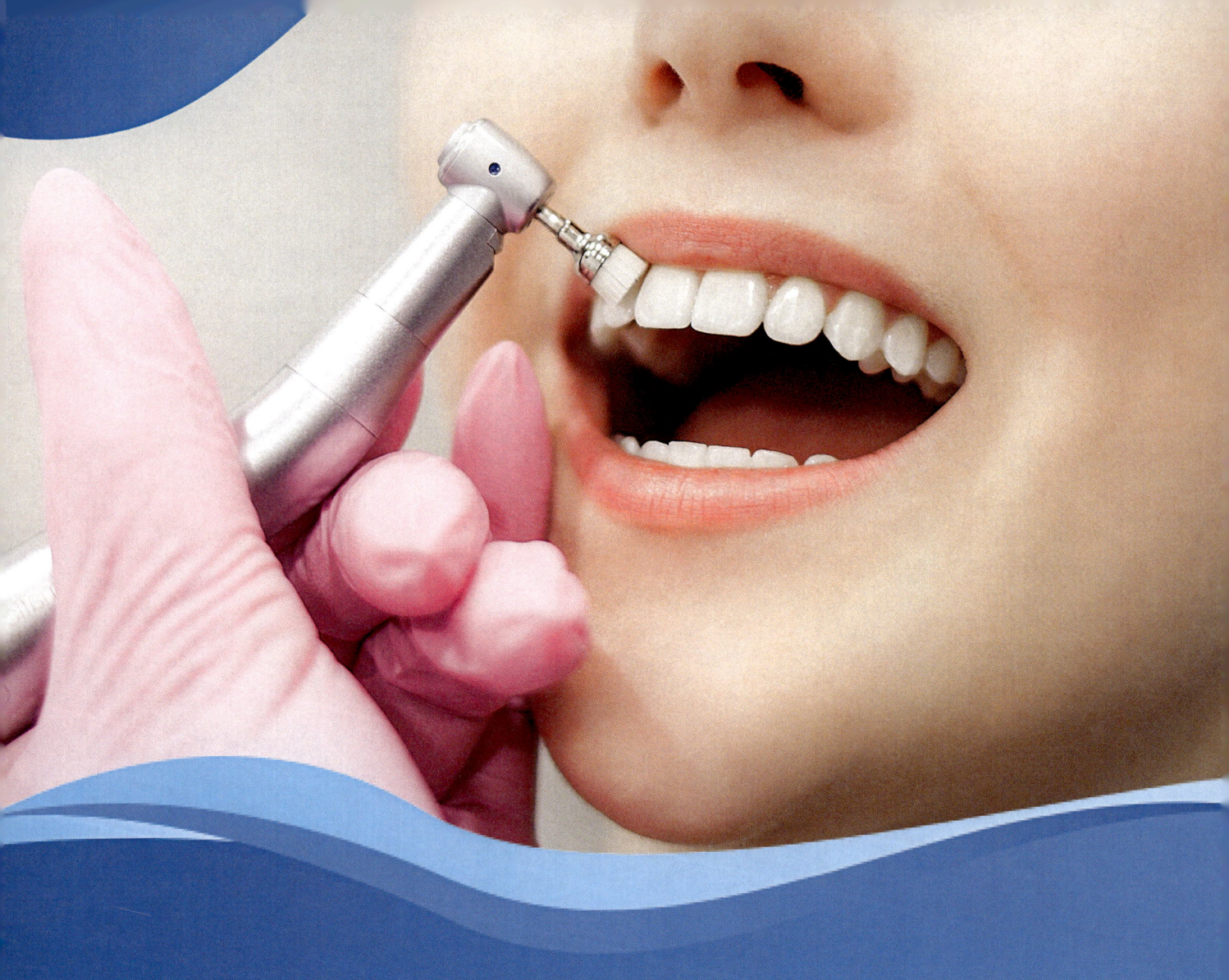

After you pick your toothpaste, the dentist cleans your teeth with a toothbrush that makes a buzzing sound.

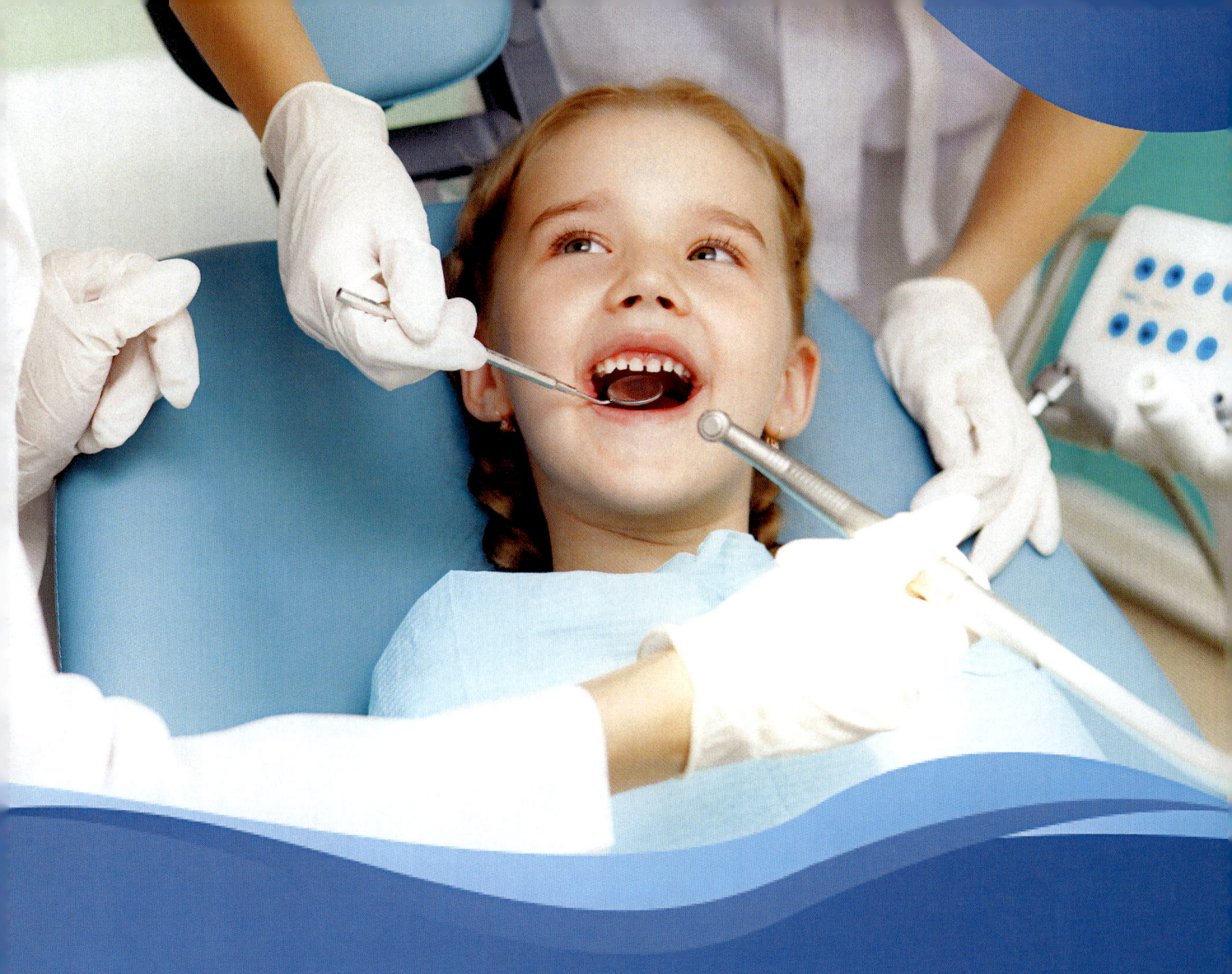

It might feel bumpy or tickle a little bit. Be sure to open wide and say "ahhh!"

While they are cleaning, they use a little squirt gun to spray water in your mouth and a straw to suck the water out.

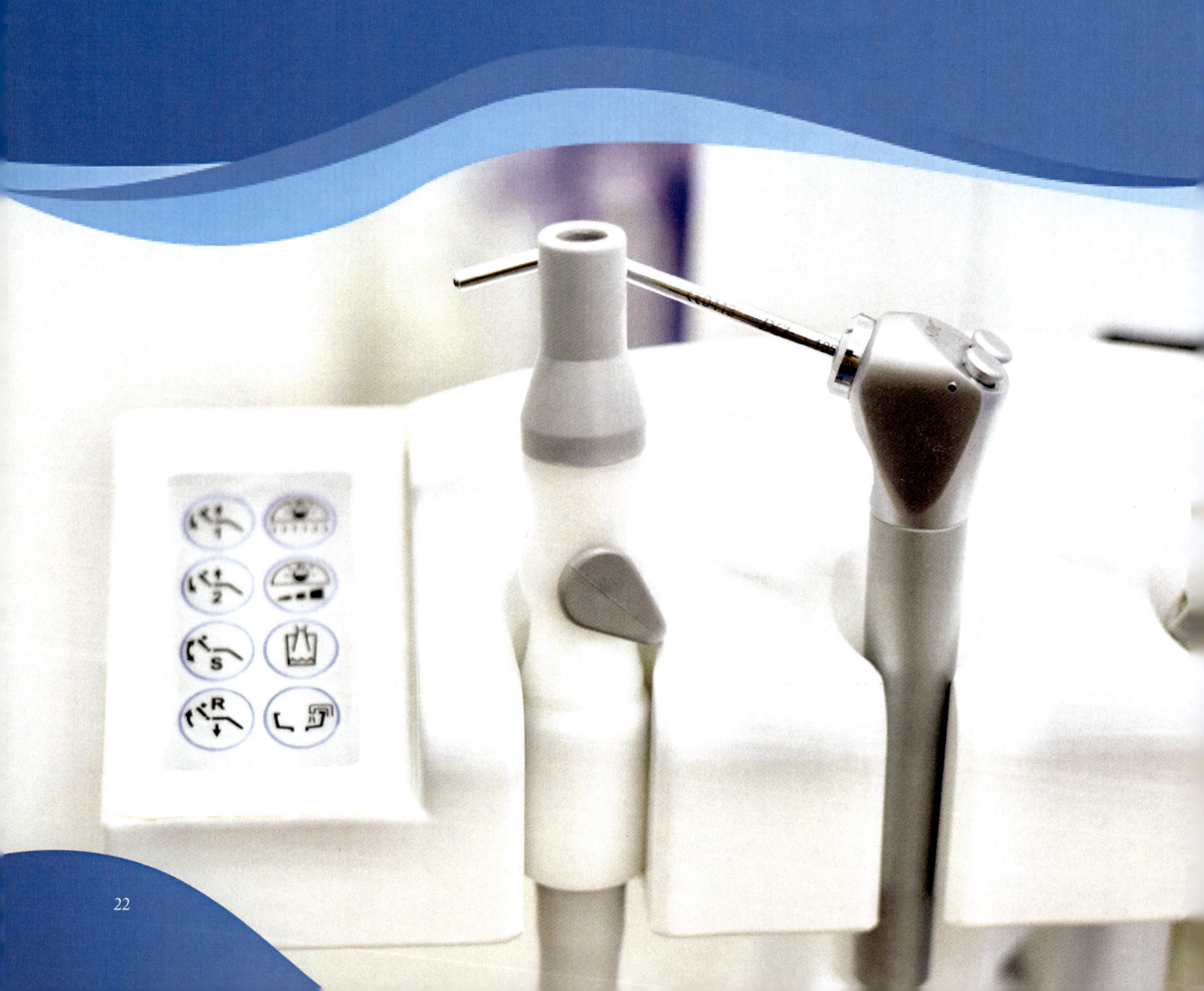

Finally, the dentist brushes fluoride on your teeth to protect them from cavities. Cavities are tiny boo-boos on your teeth.

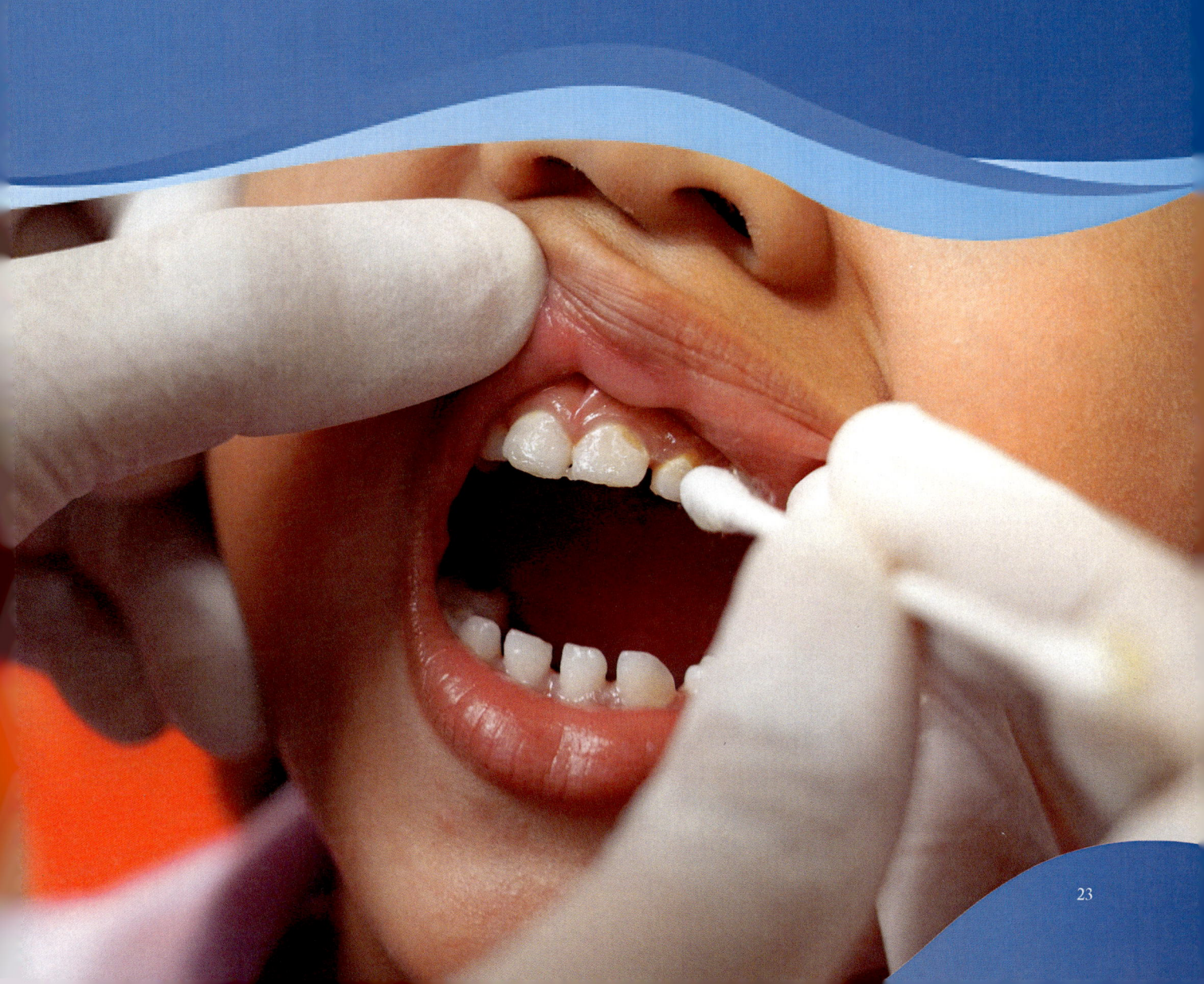

Hooray! You did it! Time to pick a prize and say goodbye until next time.